the

Art

of *Remembering*™

by

Adina L. Ruskin

For my husband,
Carl Anthony Carvalho,
with love, gratitude, and devotion.

*I have been blessed with a
wonderful family and dear friends.*

*To those here, to those on the other side,
and to those yet to come,
thank you for making my life a great adventure.*

THE ART OF REMEMBERING was produced by Asa Productions, Inc. and premiered at the 50th Edinburgh Festival Fringe, at The Roman Eagle Lodge (Stuart Stocks, Venue Manager) in Edinburgh, Scotland, in August, 1996. It was directed and choreographed by Alyssa Kennedy; the backdrop was designed and created by Betina Pels; the lighting and graphic designs were by Carl A. Carvalho; the original music was composed and recorded by John Purcell; the music was performed by John Purcell, Paul Handelman and Mark Kaufman; additional choreography was by Martita Goshen. The cast was as follows:

REBECCA..Holli Harms
BECKY...Jennifer Knipe-Blaine
REBA ....Adina L. Ruskin

THE ART OF REMEMBERING was developed at Alice's Fourth Floor Participating Artists' May Plays, in New York City, in May, 1994. It directed by Adina L. Ruskin. The cast included Magda Lang, Molly Powell and Melinda Wade. It then received a workshop production at the Trocadero in New York City, in March, 1995. It was directed by Rachel Wineberg. The cast included Louise Favier, Adina L. Ruskin and Connie Winston.

THE ART OF REMEMBERING

Rebecca remembers how she cleaned out her childhood closet while at home to bury her father. Within the objects she finds embedded stories of courage, laughter, and wisdom. Rebecca is portrayed by three actresses who represent different aspects of herself, and in turn they all play the numerous characters that arise in the memories. Rebecca is the actual physical being. Becky is the practical, somewhat skeptical one. Reba is the gutsy, take-life-by-the-horns-and-run type. Though they represent aspects of Rebecca, they are by no means one dimensional. The three actresses should wear simple, flexible outfits. We wore black Lycra pants and Lycra tops, each top in a different solid color. Our goal was to be comfortable, elegant, and to emphasize that the three are one person. There are no costume changes. All characters are created with body shifts, accents, etc. Because of the organic nature of the play, and because we are often taught to ignore the stage directions, I have decided to describe the essence of what we set out to do in each scene in a short narrative preceding each section, including specific stage directions when I simply can't control myself. Please keep in mind that improvisation, sense memory, and other theatre games can be a useful tool to enhance your production of this play. Original lighting can also be effective and if you would like a copy of the original music composed for the play, you can write to us at Asa Productions, Inc. at the address on the copyright page. One final note: There is no type casting for this play. The three women can be any combination of ethnicity, color, or age.

The stage is simple and almost bare. Upstage center, there is a large old metal trunk with labels from old time resort hotels. Surrounding the trunk are objects — several books, photo albums, jewelry boxes, loose papers, a Spanish fan, a cigar box, one elegant woman's high heel shoe, and a large blue cloth. During the course of the play the blue cloth is used as a shawl, to convert the suitcases into a gravestone, as a child's toy, as the rain, a puddle, a baby, and a shroud.

There are two smaller metal suitcases, one on either side of the main trunk downstage on a diagonal from center. The backdrop is in three canvas panels. Each panel is ten feet by four feet four inches and is painted blue — a blue that can either be the sky or the sea. Floating in this wash of blue are objects from the various memories painted on it in trompe l'oeil *style.*

As the audience enters to house music, the stage is in a half light. Rebecca is sitting in front of the trunk deciding what to repack and what to throw out, allowing each object to effect her. Stage left, Reba is sitting on the left side of her suitcase. Stage right, Becky is sitting on the left side of her suitcase. Becky and Reba are handling invisible objects, allowing the objects to effect them. This continues until the audience is seated.

Opening music begins and lights brighten.

In the beginning and ending of this first scene, the three woman, seated in the same position, move their upper bodies in unison. They all speak fragments of the sentences simultaneously as indicated. This is done to help establish that they are actually one person. Rebecca laughs as a cue and they all pick up the high heel shoe. Once again, Becky and Reba are working with invisible objects throughout this scene.

REBECCA.   13 rue Amelot, *(In unison.)* Paris, France 75011
REBA.   *(In unison.)* Paris, France 75011
BECKY.   *(In unison.)* 75011 *(They place the shoes in the cases.)*
REBECCA.   254 West End Avenue, New York City, New York 10023 *(They pick up the bundle of letters.)*
REBA.   *(In unison.)* New York City

BECKY. *(In unison.)* New York 10023 *(They place the bundle of letters in the cases.)*

REBECCA. Husiatyn, Poland *(They pick up the blue cloth.)*

REBA. Husiatyn, Poland *(Remaining seated, each actress begins their own movements, handling various objects and placing them in their cases. The blue cloth is not put in the trunk but left beside it, R. Several objects are never packed, but left very close to the trunk.)*

BECKY. Brumath, Alsace, France

REBECCA. 13 rue Amelot, Paris, France 75011

REBA. 41 Palermo, Buenos Aires, Argentina

REBECCA. 33 Elm Street, Dayton, Ohio

BECKY. 7 Calle Bella Vista, Nerja Malaga, Spain

REBA. Plaza de Potro, Cordoba, Spain

BECKY. 9 Alexander Platz, East Berlin, East Germany

REBECCA. Husiatyn, Poland

REBA. 245 West End Avenue, New York City, New York 10023

BECKY. *(Looking straight ahead.)* Who said concrete and metal cannot speak?

REBA. *(Looking straight ahead.)* Every square inch holds the memories of a thousand souls. *(Here there is a slight pause for each woman to notice a piece of paper in front of her, moving in unison, they pick up the piece of paper with their right hands, unfold it, go to tear it, stop, fold the paper, and with their hands in a prayer-like fashion, they bring the paper to their hearts. Moving their right arms in a slow poetic arc, they throw the paper into their cases and slam them shut.)*

AIRPLANE

In this story, the center trunk is used as two airplane seats. Reba will play a flight attendant miming emergency evacuation procedures, a police officer, and an old Jewish man in a New York deli. Becky will play Rachel, the protagonist of this story.

REBA. *(While latching her suitcase and getting up, she addresses the audience.)* Planes are a great place to make friends, lasting or fleeting. It's a great place to confide deep secrets to strangers and to exchange old and new stories. *(Taking up her suitcase, she moves U.L. and becomes a flight attendant, showing emergency evacuation procedures. Becky, carrying her suitcase, approaches the flight attendant for help finding her seat.)*

REBECCA. *(To audience, sitting on the airplane seat.)* When I was 17 I took a plane by myself for the first time. I was already adept at meeting people of all ages on planes, including pilots and co-pilots, in my devil adorable years. But this trip in the summer of '81 was unique, it was a maiden voyage and I prayed for days to be sitting next to Prince Charming, who wouldn't?! I had someone I cannot recollect to my left. *(Becky steps in front of Rebecca to get to her seat, carrying her suitcase with her.)* A friendly woman around my mother's age to my right. Neither was Romeo. After I got over feeling unlucky, I began to converse with the woman to my right. *(During this monologue, Becky lifts an invisible airplane window blind, looks out, and then closes it.)* I've blocked out her name, so for the sake of the story I will call her Rachel. Something about my memory of her reminds me of a Rachel. She was large, strong, and determined, to my little, strong, and determined. We were fast friends. After dinner, and probably half of my life story, she said, …

BECKY. I was a young girl, not even 10 years old when the war broke out. We lived in Paris though my parents were originally from Poland. My father was a small man with a sly smile and a gift. The gift to understand the … the unknowable, a gift to hear his intuition, to trust it I suppose, a gift to see. The Germans invaded Paris.

REBECCA. *(To the audience.)* I grew accustomed to her voice. All other sounds warmed and melted into the persistent humming of the aircraft.

BECKY. One night when father came in to say goodnight, he lingered by the side of my bed and then he said, 'Rachel my little angel, I've never lied to you, *n'est-ce pas?* And I'm always right, *n'est-ce pas?* So listen very closely. The world has gone crazy for a while, and bad things are going on. Tomorrow morning … early … the police will come for us. I have already packed my bag. But you, your sisters, and Mother will hide in the false back of our closet. I will say you are in the country visiting your Aunt. They will be satisfied and they will take me away. But no matter where they take me or whatever happens, I will survive. I promise you I will see you again. It might not be for a long time, maybe even thirty years. But don't be afraid my little angel, I love you.'

The next morning my mother woke us before dawn. We all hugged and kissed, then father insisted we hide. It seemed forever, our breath grew hot and the little air sticky ... then pounding at the door. My father answered. He asked what he had done.

REBA. *(From where she is, as police officer.)* 'All foreign Jews are to report to the precinct.'

BECKY. They asked for us. We held our breath. They searched the apartment. They left. With my father.

Well, the years passed, the war ended, no news. My family, we moved to America and we prospered in a suburb of New York City. Last month, my mother and I were on a shopping spree in the city. We decided to lunch in one of those little Kosher delis, you know, where the waiters tell you what to eat. My mother was facing the door, I was facing her, she turned white. I asked her what was wrong. She didn't say a thing. I turned around and saw nothing of interest. Then she said, ...

REBECCA. The man at the last table is wearing the suit your father was wearing the day they took him away.

BECKY. I insisted she was imagining it. She remained pale. So I got up, *(Gets up and walks over to Reba who is still U.L. and who has slowly shrunk, transforming herself into a little old man, drinking a glass of water.)* walked over to this total stranger and said, 'Excuse me sir, I know this is ridiculous, but my mother thinks you are wearing a suit that belongs to my father and of course ...

REBA. *(In a Yiddish accent.)* Moishe.

BECKY. *(Maintaining eye contact with Reba.)* His eyes brightened.

REBA. 'Moishe, how is he? Yes, of course this was his suit. He gave it to me the last time I saw him. The last time I saw him ... the day the Russians liberated our camp. *(Reba as the old man reaches out to embrace Becky. She moves away abruptly. Reba holds the half embrace as if caught in time.)*

BECKY. By this time I was pale. My father was alive or at least he survived the war. What kept him from returning?

REBECCA. Rachel paused.

BECKY. What kept him from returning? *(Pause.)* I don't know. *(Returns back to airplane seat.)* But that's why I am here tonight flying back to France after thirty years. I'm determined ...

REBECCA. Over the P.A. system ...

REBA. *(Breaks her frozen pose, becoming the flight attendant, and speaks in a French accent.)* Please fasten your seat belts, we are making our decent to Paris Roissy Charles de Gaulle. The temperature ...

REBECCA. A hush swooped down into my heart as she scribbled her address on a piece of paper, so I might write to her someday and find out if she found him, her father. *(Becky writes a mimed note, unfastens her seat belt, touches Rebecca tenderly, and gets up. Becky and Reba pick up their suitcases and walk U., put down their suitcases in unison, and stand with their backs to the audience.)* Well, time passed and I moved to Paris. Nearly five years ago my father died on his sixtieth birthday. I flew home. My father, Benjamin, was a big man with a sly smile and a gift. The gift of generosity, the gift of honesty, of love. After we buried my father, I stayed at my mother's for almost two months. My mother had been pleading with me to clean out my closet, and store my books and things in her basement. So I began to sift through the piles of things to give away, and those that must be kept: love letters wrapped with ribbon, boxes of old photos, watches long ago broken, *(Becky and Reba slowly turn to face the audience. All three women are holding an invisible piece of paper in their right hands.)* when I came across Rachel's address. I held it tight. I paused. Then I put the address back into my mess. *(The three women release their pieces of paper in unison in a fluid poetic gesture. Music comes up. Lights change.)*

THE SECRET OF LOSS

This sequence is almost dream-like. Rebecca is allowing her feelings to create random associations with the past and the loss of her father. Use simple movements that become playful. At the end of this scene, each woman should end up frozen in an attempt to embrace the other. For example, Rebecca can reach out to embrace Becky from behind just at the moment that Becky bends as if to pick something up. Each woman ending the scene on a different plane — standing, crouching, kneeling.

BECKY.   When someone passes on ...

REBECCA.   Dies ...

REBA.   yes, dies ...

REBECCA.   it's like a part of me ...

REBA.   a part of time ...

BECKY.   stands still ...

REBA.   It creates a time warp ...

REBECCA.   a passage of light ...

BECKY.   something stands still ...

REBECCA.   His body has been in the ground ...

REBA.   nearly five years ...

BECKY.   seems just ...

REBA.   that I can hear him say ...

REBECCA.   Above all else, to thine own self be true ...

REBA.   Then once he sighed and added with a twinkle ...

REBECCA.   Well, considering how Polonius and Laertes end up, perhaps you should also remember to take advice with a grain of ...

BECKY.   salt ...

REBA.   sand ...

REBECCA.   chocolate.

REBA.   That Anna was playing poker and blackjack ...

REBECCA.   For money.

BECKY.   That we were playing by the well ...

REBECCA.   Eating radish sandwiches ...

BECKY. Dad took the diesel Buick to be fixed ...

REBA. yet again ...

BECKY. This is before diesel engines were popular. So it spent a lot of time visiting the mechanic.

REBA. *(Assumes character and accent of a New England mechanic.)* So, what's wrong with it now?

REBECCA. *(As the father.)* Well, it's hot, it shakes, and it won't move.... Looks like meningitis to me. *(They all laugh heartily, overdoing it, then stop abruptly.)*

BECKY. Already five years.

REBA. Only five years.

BECKY. Already fifteen.

REBA. Only forty years.

BECKY. Already forty years are breathed parallel.

REBECCA. This is the secret.

BECKY. The secret ...

REBECCA. of loss. *(The three women dissolve out of their final pose rolling backwards and laughing.)*

NEW YEAR'S EVES

This next scene has the feeling of a slumber party in which the girls are playing games. Rebecca can begin by laying across the trunk with Reba and Becky slightly in front on either side.

REBECCA. What is the first thing I think of ... let's say ...

REBA. January first.

REBECCA. Kissing a bunch of strangers, feeling like you have to be doing something memorable.

BECKY. Not another year already.

REBA. For me it's a new start.

REBECCA. I'd rather forget most of my New Year's Eves.

REBA. Reflect, move on.

REBECCA. I was stood up in a disco parking lot. It was New Year's Eve 1978.

BECKY and REBA. I remember.

14

REBECCA.   Grandmother Frances was born on January first, at the moment between 1896 and 1897. I wish her a happy birthday just after singing "Auld Lang Syne." If I remember.

REBA.   She was a 120 when she died.

BECKY.   Well ... *(Becky and Reba start humming quietly "Auld Lang Syne." Each woman continues humming when not speaking.)*

REBECCA.   At some point she figured it made sense to lie up — 120, not bad for an old girl. You could hear her kick up her heels with her smile. Not bad for an old girl.

BECKY.   Grandfather died on January first, before I was born. So every New Year I'd hear the story how he died saving a Rembrandt painting from a fire ... *(Humming ends.)*

REBA.   On New Year's Eve.

REBECCA.   Was he burnt?

REBA.   No, heart failure.

BECKY.   *(A little bitter.)* He saved the painting.

REBA.   *(A sense of deep loss, but not bitter.)* Yes, but I often wonder if it was a fair trade.

BECKY.   *(To Reba, as if to cheer her up.)* Life's but a shadow, a poor player, that struts and frets his hour upon the stage ... *(This next sequence is done as a childish game.)*

REBECCA.   Mac.... The Scottish play, Lord M. *(They all laugh playfully.)*

REBA.   A plague o' both your houses!

REBECCA.   Mercutio, *Romeo and Juliet.*

BECKY.   The quality of mercy is not strained.

REBECCA.   Portia, *The Merchant of Venice.*

REBA.   After life's fitful fever, we shall sleep perchance to dream ...

REBECCA.   Hamlet, *Hamlet, Prince of Denmark.*

REBA.   All right. *(Becky and Reba move U. to trunk. Reba faces left while Becky picks up the blue cloth.)*

REBECCA.   *(Faces the audience.)* The last two weeks of her life, my grandmother would only quote Shakespeare. On her last breath, I could swear I heard her say ...

BECKY.   Anna ...

REBECCA.   then someone chuckled ... *(Reba chuckles.)* perchance? ...

BECKY.   Anna ... *(Reba turns toward Becky, who places the blue cloth around her.)*
REBA.   *(To Becky.)* Anna.... My name is Anna.

ANNA

In this scene, Reba as Anna establishes the character of the great-grandmother. The smaller suitcases are stacked by Rebecca and Becky to create a chair for Anna. While Anna tells her story, Rebecca and Becky listen in various positions as adoring grandchildren might.

REBA.   My name is Anna. I came to the United States at 13.
REBECCA.   In a large boat!
REBA.   Naturally.
BECKY.   3rd Class?
REBA.   Naturally. *(Sits.)* I left my hometown, Husiatyn, in ...
REBECCA.   Husiatyn, where's that? *(The girls lay down, facing their grandmother. Their positions form the shape of a boat.)*
REBA.   It's in Poland.
BECKY.   Poland ...
REBA.   It was Poland then, part of the Austrio-Hungarian empire.
BECKY.   Where is it now?
REBA.   In the Ukraine, near the Rumanian border. We were nothing more than a village by the Dniester River, cold in winter, sweltering in summer. The soil was good. We were a town of Jews and Gypsies. There was even a rumor I might be part Gypsy. I've always been keen to that notion. I suppose I left with mixed feelings. But as soon as I saw the ship, I was excited! I was the first member of my immediate family going to America. Some man had paid for the ticket.
REBECCA.   You traveled alone.
REBA.   I was 13. The bunks were lined ten high. I'm agile so I took the top bunk. *(Starts to sway back and forth.)* It turned out to be lucky. I'll spare you the details, but this was the first time at sea for most of us. I didn't get seasick. I loved it. I helped

people cook their meals. So many families took me in, fed me. *(Stands.)* One day while exploring the ship, I met a gentleman. *(She extends her hand as if to shake hands with someone. Her hand turns as if being kissed instead.)* He invited me to lunch in First Class! He thought I was beautiful and witty — and I was — so I lunched with him every day until we docked.

BECKY. Did you really?

REBA. Well, it's what I remember. When I think of Husiatyn my elbows ache. The year was 1891. *(Rebecca and Becky stand. Rebecca embraces Reba from behind and then removes the blue cloth, placing it over the suitcases to create a grave. She then kneels beside it on both knees.)*

BRUMATH

In this scene, the three women will end up kneeling around the grave, placing their hands on the stone and, then in unison, they will bend forward as if drawn into the grave. When they roll out of this position, they will be enacting a memory of the grandmother that is buried in this grave.

BECKY. My maternal grandmother came from Brumath. It's a small city in eastern France.

REBECCA. In Alsace.

BECKY. Yes! Grandmother came from there and she's buried there — on the top of a hill overlooking pastures and vineyards. It's an exclusive, gated community, for a few privileged stones. Each stone containing behind it's shinny black slate, densely packed memories. It's really a beautiful spot, ...

REBA. for the dead, ... *(Kneels.)*

BECKY. and for those left behind. I visit often. I walk down the sunlit leaves almost to the end and to the left, Blanche *(Rebecca puts her hands on the grave.)* Hermann *(Reba puts her hands on the grave.)* Klein. *(Becky kneels and puts her hands on the grave.)* I catch myself speaking out loud. Speaking out loud to her. I realize I have always been talking to her, who she is, ...

REBA. and who she was, ...

17

REBECCA. and who she will be ...

BECKY. is a part of me. *(They all bow their heads down onto the grave and hold this moment for a few beats. Then they melt from this pose, falling into each other, laughing as children.)* The sound of a well pumping ...

REBA. The laughter on Sunday afternoons ...

REBECCA. Glistening.

BECKY. We were nine children and on Sundays mother would let us have tea in the backyard. We'd rush to the well to get water, trying not to spill it, mother was strict.

REBECCA. All her copper pots hung over our heads, brighter and shinier than mid-summer.

REBA. We ate radish sandwiches ...

REBECCA. Oh no not the red kind ...

BECKY. ... in those days we ate the large root kind, sliced very thin, with butter and brown bread. It was very special, and we'd laugh ... *(They all sing "Sur le pont d'Avignon."* Becky and Reba rush to get the blue cloth and begin to play a game such as London Bridge, with Rebecca running under it each time it bellows in the air. The singing stops as music begins for the next piece. The cloth now suspended in the air comes down like the rain. Becky and Reba shake the cloth on the ground to create the effect of a puddle.)*

RAIN

In Rain *we used simple, somewhat literal movements that capture the sense of freedom and loss. We had Reba jump onto the cases as if she might leap off a cliff, instead she opens up her arms and spirit in thanks to the rain. This quality of opening up is essential to this segment. Some of the movement can be in unison.*

REBECCA. Is it the sight of the rain that makes me remember the evening I danced barefoot ...

* See Special Note on Songs and Recordings on copyright page.

18

REBA.   I wanted to save my shoes ...
BECKY.   Or is it the sound of the hammering in plucks ...
REBA.   pulucs ...
BECKY and REBA.   pusshhhs ...
BECKY.   ... against the glimmering pavement or the smell of the trees coming to life as the rain shakes them to their senses, that makes you remember that night I ...
REBA.   Sat at the window and cried because, no matter how hard I tried, time would never stand still and ...
BECKY.   Danced, I hadn't planned to, just leapt right into the air, my hair clinging to my face, I ...
REBA.   *(Suddenly leaping onto the cases.)* Thought he could never ...
REBECCA.   Die ...
BECKY.   Father, how could he ...
REBECCA.   Bastard!
REBA.   I spun with the rain as if I were the breath I breathed ...
BECKY.   Not noticing the tears ...
REBA.   The rain had freed my soul ... *(Rebecca and Becky pick up the blue cloth and place it over Reba's shoulders.)*
BECKY and REBA.   *(Echoed.)* Soul ...
BECKY and REBA.   And I saved my shoes ... *(Rebecca and Becky offer a hand to Reba who steps down as Anna.)*

ANNA II

REBA.   The year was 1891. I arrived in America to find myself engaged to a man I never met. He offered me gold coins. I said no. I simply said no. *(Sits.)* No one buys me. Most girls never thought of saying no.
REBECCA.   Where did you go?
REBA.   I stayed with an awful old aunt and started rolling cigars for 60¢ a week. My first job in America. I worked overtime. I managed to save enough to bring over my brother, Joe. Little by little we brought over the whole family, and eventually the whole town. Aaron set up a free loan society for anyone from

Husiatyn.

REBECCA. Aaron?

REBA. Ahh, Aaron was the love of my life. We were both six-teen when we met. My aunt locked me in my room when I told her I was going to marry him.

REBECCA. No!

REBA. Yes. For six weeks. I managed to slide down the fire es-cape and Aaron and I eloped. Your grandmother Frances was born a year later. We were so close in age that later in life she would call me Anna and not Mother.

BECKY. Anna ...

REBECCA. What did Aaron do?

REBA. His family was in the tobacco business, so we were in the tobacco business. *(She goes to caress Becky's face and freezes in motion.)*

REBECCA. *(To the audience.)* My father used to tell me how Anna rolled cigars for 60¢ a week. And on her way home from work, she'd walk through Grand Central Station just to feel.... The station had marble floors ...

REBA. And I'd stop under the big old clock and watch all the hellos and good-byes. If the guard wasn't watching, I'd go down to one of the tracks and put my two hands on the iron. I'd lean my cheek against the cold metal and breath deep the scent of adventure. So one day I went up to the teller and asked how far can two adults and a baby go for five dollars.

BECKY. *(As teller.)* 'Dayton, Ohio, Ma'am.'

REBA. So we moved to Dayton, Ohio. When we got there we discovered there were no other Jews. And no one would buy to-bacco from us. Luckily Aaron was a Freemason and, if you're a Mason, you're accepted. So we did fairly well. Frances went to parochial school. We had a little house with fruit trees. I planted a garden — the soil was good. The year was ... *(At some point during this monologue, Rebecca and Becky have stood up. During Reba's last line they remove the blue cloth together — gently — and it is this action that makes Anna vanish and Reba return.)*

20

THE SECRET OF LOSS REPRISE

They return to The Secret of Loss *and here we also used simple movements to create the image.*

BECKY.   Already ...
REBECCA.   Only five years ...
REBA.   Already ... *(Reba stands as Rebecca and Becky place the blue cloth over the cases, creating another grave.)*
BECKY.   His body has been in the ground ...
REBECCA.   Walking along, *(They all individually walk in a wide circle.)* my arm swings above my head. *(Reba reaches with her left hand up toward D.L.)* I can almost reach. *(Rebecca reaches with her left hand up toward D.L.)* I skip on my tippytoes to cling to his hand. *(Becky reaches with her left hand up toward D.L.)* It's the scent of peaches, juicy, that makes me remember. *(All hands come down.)* We were on our way to the fruit stand. Father talked of Darwin that day. He was very sensible.
BECKY.   Only fifteen ...

ANNA III

This is the only Anna scene where Reba does not wear the blue cloth as a shawl, but instead picks it up as if it were her baby.

REBA.   The year was ... *(She walks around cases, picking up the cloth as if it were a baby.)* I lost a baby in a careless childbirth accident. I heard him cry, but I was too weak to hold him. The next morning when I awoke, they told me he was dead. *(The women are in a diagonal line facing the audience. Rebecca and Becky now have mimed babies in their arms as well. In unison, they all step forward, kneel, and release the baby. Reba leaves the cloth on the floor. They step back.)* I decided it was time to move on. We went back to New York. *(In unison, they each pivot, returning to face front. Lights shift.)*

FRUIT STANDS

In Fruit Stands, *we stood very still creating a deep sense of isolation, pivoting in quarter turns now and then to emphasize a link, a listening.*

REBECCA.   It's the fruit stands that startle me most.

REBA.   Already twenty years. *(Pivots to face R.)*

REBECCA.   I'm mesmerized by the color.

BECKY.   That is the secret ... *(Pivots to face L.)*

REBECCA.   Each fruit plump ...

REBA.   The secret of loss ...

REBECCA.   And oh, the scent. I had been on holiday in Leningrad with my closest girlfriend. I hadn't noticed at first the lack of color, of fresh foods, the smells, how long had my senses been deprived — a week, not even.

She called me Sarah. My name isn't Sarah. *(Pivots to face R.)*

BECKY.   *(Pivoting at the same time as Rebecca, to face forward.)* Sarah, ...

REBECCA.   She said, her eyes looking down, beautiful, despite her hunched shoulders.

BECKY.   I was singled out by Mengele for scientific research. I was beautiful and naked, so I threw myself at a young guard's feet. I'm not proud nor ashamed.

REBECCA.   He called me Pedro. My name isn't Pedro. *(Rebecca and Reba pivot at the same time to face forward.)*

REBA.   I'm a lawyer. For three generations my family have been fighting corruption, and in Argentina this makes you a radical, one step above a rebel. In 1968, I was appointed head of the prison system. I quit. I'm not proud ... *(Rebecca pivots to face R.)*

BECKY.   Proud or ashamed. I'm alive — beautiful to be alive! The Russians liberated our camp in 1945. They raped the young women — young — I'm not sure how they knew which women were young. I was never angry with them. You see Sarah, they liberated us ... *(Rebecca pivots to face front.)*

REBA.   A Chief Warden, no, I quit, only to find myself six

months later a prisoner. They left me alone in the "interview chamber" to get the "interviewer." Life as a public figure and I've never gotten used to interviews. So in the five minutes I was carelessly left alone I ate my address book — yes, from Adler to Zilberfain. You see Pedro, I could no longer control my own fate, but I could improve the chances for my friends ...

BECKY. *(She pivots to face R.)* Sarah are you married? Engaged? I've been very happy. I have a good husband and we depend on each other. No, I'm not telling you to forget, but you have to live fully, joyfully, in remembering the dead. In a way you are living for them. And to be happy is to say to those who do evil, 'You have failed.' Remember, evil spelled backwards is live! Are you married? Engaged? No? Dear, such a beautiful girl, find a husband and be happy.

REBECCA. I will Sarah, I will.

REBA. *(Pivots to face L.)* From Adler to Zilberfain — boy were they annoyed. Torture? Yes, but worse than torture is the fear, the fear that they'll hurt your wife and children. One's own pain is always easier to bare. Whose responsible? Greed. Fear. No it's not easy to move on, but all you can do is keep striving ... for the light.

REBECCA. It was the fruit stand that made me think of Sarah and Pedro, yes. *(Pause.)*

ANNA IV

This scene has a great deal of commedia dell'arte and light-heartedness. The grandchildren go from playing cards on the suitcases to straddling them as chairs while Anna relives her vibrant past.

REBA. *(Reba as Anna breaks the silence with a big laugh as she picks up the blue cloth and throws it around her shoulders. The grand-children sit by the cases as if playing cards.)* I would never have come to America — not in a million years — if I ever thought they'd outlaw gambling. Gambling, *(She cuts the cards for the kids.)* outlawed in America — puritanical twits. After Aaron died and I retired, I got more serious about my hobbies: Knitting, reading, and gambling. The year was 1944, La Guardia was Mayor of New York, and he decided that such high spirited games were against the law. Well, we continued to play regardless ... some people were shocked that a group of 60-year-old women played blackjack and poker for money. Puf! One time your father, my grandson, came to pick me up. He was such a good boy, only he was a little absent minded. He was probably thinking of girls, so he forgot the secret knock. *(The grandchildren do the secret knock against the cases.)* We threw our cards and chips into my voracious knitting basket. A few of us would start to do our knitting while the rest looked like they were making tea! Ha! I was afraid some of the old girls would kill him. Personally I had a pair of eights, mind you I was a good bluffer.

BECKY. Secret knock? Aren't you exaggerating?

REBA. Are you kidding? The police didn't have anything better to do then raid our gambling clubs.

REBECCA. Clubs?

REBA. That's what we called it. It was just Betty's apartment. Once, Tillie The Texan — she was my oldest and dearest friend — she got sore because she lost, so she ratted on us. *(They all act out the story in a commedia dell'arte fashion. Rebecca plays the cop banging at the door. Becky plays the cop barring passage through the window.)* The cops came banging in with a search warrant. We tried to slip out the window. They caught us on the fire escape. They booked us. *(Rebecca mimes handcuffing Reba.)*

BECKY. What happened?

REBA. I spent the night in jail. I don't recommend it.

BECKY. Anna ... what happened ...

REBA. Frances bailed me out in the morning. When we appeared before the judge he said ...

BECKY. *(As judge.)* Mrs. Aaron Reader.

REBA. Yes, Your Honor.

BECKY. *(As judge.)* I hear you have the kitty.

REBA. Oh, No Your Honor, I have no cat.

BECKY. *(As judge.)* Mrs. Reader, do not provoke me.

REBA. Young man, my son is at the front with General Patton. He's General Patton's doctor, serving his country, risking his life. He has better things to do than harass old ladies.

BECKY. *(As judge.)* Case dismissed! Dismissed! *(Rebecca and Becky straddle suitcases once more.)*

REBA. I guess I'm a gambling spirit. Perhaps it's the gypsy in me: a little luck and a lot of …

REBECCA. Unmitigated gall …

REBA. The year was 1944. *(She turns to leave.)*

ALZHEIMER'S

In this scene, Rebecca becomes Tillie The Texan, one of her great-grandmother's colorful friends, recounting her wild past. It is not until the very end of the scene that we discover that Tillie's friend has Alzheimer's.

REBECCA. Anna don't go. Not yet. Dad always told me one of your stories at bedtime. Tell me about Tillie The Texan.

REBA. Not again.

REBECCA. Oh, please Anna!

REBA. All right. But you'll have to help me. *(Reba, still as Anna, takes Rebecca's arm as they walk D.L.)* Tillie The Texan was …

REBECCA. A journalist!

REBA. Yes, that's right, a journalist. A spirited girl, she spent a lot of time in …

REBECCA. Spain!

REBA. We met in Nerja, thrity-one … *(They spin off of each other. Rebecca ends up with the blue cloth over one shoulder and becomes Tillie.)*

REBECCA. *(With a Texan accent.)* No! forty-one years ago.

REBA. Already? *(They stand for a moment in the same pose.)*

REBECCA. Yes, already. Nerja is a little coastal town near Malaga, Spain, where flocks of English and Germans migrate semi-annually. I'm an American. Elsa is Danish. *(She indicates Becky. Reba crosses over to Becky and stands behind her.)* We were both sitting at the bar of El Rincon, before noon. We had a lot in common, both writers, both women. *(She crosses to the others.)* The season hadn't quite begun. Nerja is the kind of town you

25

keep going back to — warm and white-washed. I was staying with a friend named Jingle ...

REBA. Jingle!?

REBECCA. His name was Jingle. Do you remember Jingle, Elsa? He was the cockney bloke who had made his first fortune as a jockey, his second racing cars and then he became a flamenco guitarist. Did we ever sleep that spring? Do you remember the dancing until two? Sevillana after sevillana.

Elsa, the practical jokes, you must remember those. What was his name, you know, that arrogant hunk, the one who thought all he had to do was snap? He was in love with the cafe owners daughter, Maria Carmen, but he didn't speak any Spanish. So we taught him to say, *'Eres mas guapa que el ano del asno.'* He thought he was saying, 'you are more beautiful than a jewel.'

REBA. What was he saying?

REBECCA. Well, he mustered all his arrogant, slimy self together, presented her with a flower and said, 'You are more beautiful than the anus of the ass.' He was flying out the door — her brothers cursing him, *'Maricón! ... Coño! ... Asno!'* — boom onto his beautiful *culo.* And Fernando, Elsa — how much in love you both were ...

(To audience.) I was in Denmark on business. I hadn't seen Elsa in years. We exchanged the occasional card, of course. So I looked her up. Her daughter explained, ... *(She returns to others and sits opposite Becky.)*

REBA. *(As Elsa's daughter.)* Mother developed Alzheimer's in her early fifties. But you can tell she's happy to see you. She gets agitated and tries to talk. She feels something when she can remember.

BECKY. Aaahh ... Evan ... Evan.

REBECCA. Yes, that was his name — that ass. *(Reba takes hold of the blue cloth, placing it over her shoulder, and walks across the stage allowing the cloth to drag along behind her.)*

REBA. *(As Anna.)* How many times have you heard that story?

REBECCA. I don't remember. *(Reba places the blue cloth on the ground as Becky begins the next scene. Whistling music — or something youthful — begins.)*

THE MANOR

The Manor is a playful piece. Rebecca remembers one of her own childhood memories. We used the two small suitcases as if they were milk canisters — the big, old fashioned kind. Then they are stacked on top of the trunk to make a hill.

BECKY. The Manor! Remember The *Manoir?*
REBA. I thought it was something out of *Madame Bovary.*
REBECCA. Yah I did.
BECKY. I hadn't read *Madame Bovary.*
REBECCA. No, I hadn't. I was very ... young.
REBA. And free.
BECKY. For the summer.
REBECCA. The local farmers, two maybe three miles away, had never seen an American.
BECKY. I had never seen a cow milked — for real — up close.
REBA. It was an even trade.
REBECCA. I was the youngest in our pack.
BECKY. So I went for the milk ...
REBECCA. Slowly ... stopping to pick wild strawberries ...
BECKY. I took the short cut there and the long way back.... Always ...
REBA. Always ...
BECKY. *(They all are sitting upon the suitcases and the trunk, stacked up to form a hill.)* Do you think there are people on other planets?
REBECCA. ... in other galaxies ...
REBA. Yah ...
REBECCA. Like Alpha Centauri.
REBA. Remember reading *Rouge Ship,* where they're on their way to ...
REBECCA. Alpha Centauri and they pass through a time warp ...
BECKY. only they don't know it and ...
REBECCA. they live up there for four generations and

when ...

REBA.   they get back only four years have passed!

REBECCA.   I suppose there could be life on other planets.

BECKY.   I had grown more tolerant.

REBECCA.   Yes.

BECKY.   At 12 I thought everything was stupid. Underneath the old pine, I said ...

REBECCA.   12, 22, what does it matter ten years experience when Camus says ...

BECKY.   'Everything is Nothing.'

REBA.   The pine tree chuckled.

BECKY.   I hated myself.

REBECCA.   At 12 I thought everything was stupid.

REBA.   15, and anything is possible. *(She leaps off the cases and the others follow. She then does a cartwheel across to L. Rebecca and Becky pick up the cases as if they were milk canisters.)*

REBECCA.   On my way back, milk canisters in hand — I'd nestle in among the tall wheat ...

BECKY.   Feeling the earth ...

REBECCA.   Watching the sky ...

BECKY.   I grow more tolerant ...

REBECCA.   I'd forget that the milk shouldn't sit in the sun ... *(Reba slowly picks up the blue cloth, places it over her shoulders, and walks D.C, passing in between Rebecca and Becky on the word "wild.")*

BECKY.   And expand in thought ... I roll over on my side and ...

REBECCA.   Whisper ...

BECKY and REBA.   Tall wheat and wild. *(The lights change and whistling music stops.)*

ANNA V

This scene takes place in a synagogue on Yom Kippur, the most solemn religious fast of the Jewish year, the last of the ten days of penitence. We had Rebecca and Becky stand on the case stage right in the act of praying. The appropriate movement is a gentle swaying, front to back, and a small bending from the

knees, occasionally rocking the upper body while striking your
chest with your fist gently in a symbolic gesture of remorse and
penance. Anna is also doing these movements while she speaks
to the audience.

REBA.   The year was 1952. I was never much for institutional
religions but, Gypsy or not, on Yom Kippur I always felt Jewish.
Guilty? For gambling?
BECKY and REBECCA.   Sssshh!
REBA.   Never! But it feels good to remember, and to know on
Yom Kippur thousands all over the world are remembering, re-
flecting, yes even praying. So I always tried to get to temple at
least on Yom Kippur.

Life had been a real adventure, but I missed Aaron so.
I went to Temple Emanuel that year and between Kol Nidre
and Yskor I let go. *(Opens arms and, after a beat, lets the blue cloth*
drop to floor.) I guess it was an impractical moment to die, but
I've always loved a little mischief. *(She falls back laughing as Re-*
becca and Becky come up behind her and catch her. They lower her to
the ground. Melancholy harmonica music comes on and lights change
to blue. Rebecca and Becky roll up the blue cloth and give it to Reba,
who has sat up. Rebecca and Becky hug as Reba puts the rolled up
cloth by the trunk. She sees a letter, discovers what it is and screams
with delight. Lights change. They all sit in a semi-circle D.C.)

BUS STOP

Bus Stop *and* Embarrassing Moments *have the feeling of*
delicious gossip. In a simple, relaxed manner each aspect of
Rebecca tries to outdo the other in remembering the most awk-
ward moments of her life.

REBA.   Oh my God, here's the love letter I taped to the bus
stop on 65th and Broadway ...
REBECCA.   Where glass and metal meet.
BECKY.   The bus was on time.

REBECCA.   But he was late.

BECKY.   Love letters written but never read ...

REBA.   Yah, but this one got posted on the bus stop. Anyone could have read ... *(Places love letter on floor in front of her. Letter remains there until the end of the play.)*

BECKY.   Still, it wasn't the most embarrassing thing I've ever done.

REBA.   That's right, there was ...

EMBARRASSING MOMENTS

REBECCA.   Oh my God! I was 22, travelling throughout Western Europe for the summer. So, I stayed mostly with friends and friends of friends. These very nice people put me up for over a week. They had a lovely guest room ...

BECKY.   Only they forgot to change the sheets.

REBECCA.   About a week later, I'm trying to be discreet. I had no clue. I had never even heard of ...

REBA.   Crabs! *(They all squeal.)*

REBECCA.   Really. I was very naive.

BECKY and REBA.   Sure!

REBECCA.   So I'm scratching my way through Holland ...

BECKY.   France ...

REBA.   Italy ...

REBECCA.   And then back to France. It never dawned on me. Two months later after a shower I scratch and up comes ... with claws and everything. *(They all squeal.)* I had met up with my parents. My mother and I go to the drugstore and she asks the pharmacist, *(Facing the audience.)* 'What's best for killing parasites?'

REBA.   *(Facing the audience, in a French accent.)* 'What kind Madame?'

REBECCA.   'Oh, it's for my daughter. She has CRABS.'

BECKY and REBA.   No!

REBECCA.   Yes. I wanted to melt like the wicked witch, on the spot. Why couldn't she have said it was for a friend?

BECKY.   That was truly embarrassing.

REBECCA.   Yah.

BECKY.   But the most humiliating moment was in a video store. You see I had never seen a porno movie ...

REBECCA.   I was 25.

BECKY.   I figured every adult should have seen at least one porno film ...

REBA.   Of course.

BECKY.   OK. *(They all get up and walk around as if in a video store.)* I walk into this video store, feeling like Woody Allen. Excuse me, umm ...

REBA.   *(Facing the audience, as video clerk.)* Yah, can I help you?

BECKY.   *(Standing C., facing the audience.)* I'd like ... I look around the store. It's almost empty. I'd like to rent a porno film, only I've never rented one before, so can you suggest something?

REBA.   *(As clerk.)* Nope.

BECKY.   Excuse me?

REBA.   *(As clerk.)* Never seen one myself.

BECKY.   Right, this guy has never seen a porno film. He probably acts in them.

REBA.   *(As clerk.)* But you can look through this catalogue.

REBECCA.   No!

BECKY.   It gets worse. I look through the catalogue: *Emmanuel, Virgins of the Night, A Visit to the Pediatrician.* I mean really.

REBECCA.   *(Facing the audience.)* So what did I pick?

BECKY.   *An Adventure in Bondage.*

BECKY and REBA.   No!

BECKY.   I'm so embarrassed.... So, I ask the guy for the movie. But I hadn't noticed that the store had filled up. So after saying in a brave voice, "I'd like *An Adventure in Bondage,* please," *(Rebecca and Reba freeze in a pose of sheer horror.)* I turn around to see this old lady, a couple of guys, and two young girls all starring at me. Horrified! It was just like a freeze frame out of a Woody Allen. *(They break the freeze and cross U. to sit on the trunk.)* That's probably the most embarrassing self inflicted moment of my life. *(She joins the others on the trunk.)*

REBECCA. What does that mean?

BECKY. Oh, gosh. Mother embarrassed me constantly for at least eight years.

REBA. Yup.

REBECCA. But that's normal.

BECKY. Absolutely.

REBA. Sure, but that doesn't make it less painful.

REBECCA. Just wait until I'm a mother.

BECKY. I can wait.

REBA. I know. I think if my kids do half the stupid things I did, I'll go prematurely grey.

BECKY. Don't worry, I'll have white hair anyway by the time I have kids. *(Rebecca discovers a Spanish fan.)*

REBA. *(Pointing out that she already has white hair.)* Excuse me, already.

CORDOBA

The fan Rebecca finds by the trunk triggers her personal memory of studying in Cordoba, Spain. We made this a very stylized piece with strong Spanish gestures, such as flamenco poses, toreador movements, etc. A great deal of the movements were done in unison. The scene begins with a glowing feeling and exuberance, and becomes dry, cold, and matter-of-fact. It is important not to get melodramatic so as to allow the cynicism of the piece to come through. [Remember that the play is one voice broken into three aspects, thus there are no pauses between lines except when noted.]

REBECCA. In Cordoba, there is always time ...

ALL. For a second cup of coffee ...

REBA. Time suspended in a sip ...

BECKY. Or a glance ...

REBECCA. The heal striking the stone until the history shakes loose. I spent a year studying at the University of Cordoba, Spain. I was the only American and the only Jew living in the old quarter of the city. The locals nicknamed me, "La Cordobesa."

BECKY. It was an honor. Cordoba had been the Muslim capital of Spain.

REBA. From 711 to 1318.

REBECCA. More or less.... Its mosque second only to Mecca.

BECKY. And for almost three, four-hundred years, Jews ...

REBA. Muslims ...

BECKY. Christians ...

REBECCA. Co-existed ...

REBA. Sharing ideas ...

BECKY. Literature ...

REBECCA. *(Very bubbly and innocently.)* Recipes ... *(Pause as Becky and Reba look at her like she's stupid.)*

BECKY. The stone walls and warm people of Cordoba taught me to slow down.

REBA. You can hear better when you have time for a second cup.

REBECCA. Yes, no one in Cordoba is on time. Not even Franco's General who came to speak at the University.

REBA. The General spoke of military strategy.

BECKY. Funny, he never mentioned how he would lock up a prisoner in a small cell and rip them to pieces with medieval instruments of torture.

REBA. For the fun of it.

REBECCA. He gave a nice little lecture and we sat there.

BECKY. No one wanted to be rude.

REBECCA. Military Strategic Maneuvers.

REBA. So I cornered him on his way out ...

REBECCA. and asked the gentle old grandfather ...

BECKY. how does it feel sir ...

REBA. to murder someone with your own two hands?

BECKY. His green eyes blazed into mine.

REBECCA. He patted me on the cheek ...

BECKY. and said, 'It was war' ...

REBA. 'It was war.'

REBECCA.   He clicked his heels and before ...

BECKY.   I could say ...

REBA.   my nickname is the La Cordobesa ...

BECKY.   and yours is ...

REBA.   El Carnicero.

REBECCA.   The Butcher.

BECKY.   He was gone.

REBA.   And I felt the blood on my cheek. *(Reba and Becky are facing each other with Rebecca in between them, facing front. They each take a step into each other, almost touching, then pivot out. Reba and Becky walk around their respective cases, stopping in front of them as Rebecca returns to the trunk, sits on it, and picks up a framed letter.)*

EAST BERLIN

The essence of East Berlin *is of solidarity. We could all be this young woman, for various reasons and in diverse challenges. Throughout the play there is a strong pulse uniting the three aspects of Rebecca. We used many different triangles, as well as circles to help create the oneness. However, this oneness is intended to extend to all humans, that we are all connected, and perhaps are simply different aspects of each other. This is strongly implied here by having Rebecca and Becky lip-sync the monologue, though they create no sound and should be in shadow.*

REBECCA.   *(Reading from the framed letter. She remains seated throughout the monologue.)* The Asians chose the phoenix to symbolize world peace. I've always wondered why they chose a *mythical* bird to represent peace.

REBA.   Erika, my East German pen pal, always wrote the most unusual letters. But this one, the first one, I felt it was worthy of framing.

REBECCA.   *(Reading from framed letter.)* I was born on August 15th, 1961 in East Berlin. The *Encyclopedia Britannica* ... *(Rebecca and Becky overlap their words as Becky becomes Erika, the girl who*

34

wrote the letter. Lights cross fade to focus on Becky while the others are in dimmed light. Rebecca and Reba lip-sync the words.)

BECKY. *(In a German accent.)* ...will tell you that on the night of August 12th, 1961 the East German Volkskammer "People's Chamber" decided to protect East Germany by building the Berlin Wall. Fifteen feet high — counting the barbed wire — and 103 miles long. Five thousand people managed to escape. More than that were caught trying and a 191 people died attempting to climb up and over — or at least that's how many the *Britannica* tells us.

On November 9th, 1918 Berlin became the first capital of the First German Republic. One generation later, on November 9th, 1938, Hitler's government wrought havoc — breaking shop windows and people — it would be known as Kristallnacht. So it wasn't a coincidence that on November 9th, 1981, I asked for a visa to leave the country — by doing so I was expelled from the University. I couldn't get a job. I can't remember the day mortar and brick encased me. But I remember the day I found a way out. I was one of the first East Germans to cross over into Hungary, then to Austria to get back to Berlin, West Berlin. I didn't know when I'd see my mother and sisters again — and as I hugged them good-bye, I knew for the first time, pain. I felt the heart, of the world — of the world breaking — for an instant you know the mother whose child dies in her arms; the Jew fleeing from a cattle car; the Kurd; the Armenian; all swelling in my throat, for them as much as for myself I crossed the border. I remember the fruit stands in West Berlin — all that color.

A few months later November 9th, 1989 — oh yes I remember that day — I learned what it meant to breath, to really breath, from your gut, as my mother walked through the Brandenburg gate ... *(The lights come back up on all.)*

REBECCA. *(Stands, walks D.C. still holding the framed letter in her left hand.)* It only takes one generation to forget.

REBA. *(Turning towards C.)* It only takes one generation to forget.

BECKY. *(Turning towards C.)* It only takes one generation to forget. *(Ending music begins.)*

ENDING

REBECCA.   There is the bus stop on 65th and Broadway, where glass and metal meet, *(They all bend down to pick up the love letter, which has been D.C. Rebecca actually picks up the love letter with her right hand while the others mime the action in unison.)* on whose shiny surface I taped my first love letter.

REBA.   The bus was on time.

REBECCA.   But he was late.

BECKY.   Who said concrete and metal cannot speak?

REBECCA.   Every square inch holds the memories of a thousand ... *(Over the next few lines, Becky and Reba walk U. to the trunk, pick it up, and bring it D., putting it behind Rebecca.)*

REBA.   How clearly ...

REBECCA.   a city ...

BECKY.   can speak.

REBECCA.   I wonder ...

REBA.   Husiatyn.

REBECCA.   New York.

BECKY.   Brumath.

REBA.   Dayton.

REBECCA.   Buenos Aires.

REBA.   Warsaw. *(Over the next few lines, they open the trunk and take the framed letter and the love letter from Rebecca's hands, placing them into the trunk. They all then, slowly, start to raise their arms into the air. Becky and Reba only raise their outside arms, leaving their inside hands on the lid of the trunk.)*

BECKY.   St. Petersburg.

REBECCA.   Beirut.

BECKY.   Sarajevo.

REBA.   Port au Prince.

REBECCA.   How much more articulate will these be ...

REBA.   when there no longer is a soul who remembers ... *(They all snap their arms down as the trunk slams shut.)*

BECKY.   Will the walls of the city speak? *(The lights slowly fade to black over the last few lines. Music becomes louder.)*

REBA.   Warsaw.

BECKY. St. Petersburg.
REBECCA. Addis Ababa.
BECKY. Sarajevo.
REBA. Port au Prince.
BECKY. St. Petersburg.
REBECCA. Addis Ababa.
BECKY. Sarajevo.
REBA. Warsaw.

THE END

PROPERTY LIST

High heel shoe (REBECCA)
Bundle of letters (REBECCA)
Blue cloth (REBECCA)
Piece of paper (REBECCA)
Love letter (REBA)
Spanish fan (REBECCA)
Framed letter (REBECCA)

AUTHOR'S NOTE

I am a patient optimist. I believe that we can each learn from our mistakes and that by doing so, little by little, we can collectively learn from one another. With this knowledge, it is my hope that eventually humanity will stop repeating cruel and hateful acts. THE ART OF REMEMBERING, therefore, is a tribute to memory.

Asa Productions is a non-profit arts production company. "Asa" means to create and to heal, in Hebrew, Arabic, and Aramaic. Asa Productions' mission is to create, promote, and produce art — including theatre, music and visual arts — that strives to enhance communication and understanding among peoples of different generations, cultures, races and religions.

This play is educational, easy to relate to and therefore can be used as a learning tool. If you are using it in the classroom and would like more information, I will be happy to try and answer any questions you have, and refer you to sources for more historical information about anything mentioned in the play. Please write to me c/o Asa Productions.

We at Asa Productions were touched and grateful for all the thank yous we received from students as well as people from all over the world who took the time to sign our guest book at the 50th Edinburgh Festival Fringe. We are delighted that audiences grasped and enjoyed the fact that the play is the unfolding of memories.

Adina L. Ruskin

Asa Productions is founded in tribute to and in memory of Dr. Asa P. Ruskin, a renowned physician, humanist, human rights activist, author, teacher, pilot, inventor, and a wonderful father.

SUR LE PONT D'AVIGNON
(traditional)

Sur le pont d'Avignon
L'on y danse l'on y danse

Sur le pont d'Avignon
L'on y danse tout en rond